In Mouse's Backyard

JAMES NARDI

Schiffer Books are available at special discounts for bulk purchases for sales promotions or premiums. Special editions, including personalized covers, corporate imprints, and excerpts can be created in large quantities for special needs. For more information contact the publisher:

Published by Schiffer Publishing Ltd.
4880 Lower Valley Road
Atglen, PA 19310
Phone: (610) 593-1777; Fax: (610) 593-2002
E-mail: Info@schifferbooks.com

For the largest selection of fine reference books on this and related subjects, please visit our website at **www.schifferbooks.com**
We are always looking for people to write books on new and related subjects. If you have an idea for a book please contact us at the above address.

This book may be purchased from the publisher.
Include $5.00 for shipping.
Please try your bookstore first.

You may write for a free catalog.

In Europe, Schiffer books are distributed by
Bushwood Books
6 Marksbury Ave.
Kew Gardens
Surrey TW9 4JF England
Phone: 44 (0) 20 8392 8585; Fax: 44 (0) 20 8392 9876
E-mail: info@bushwoodbooks.co.uk
Website: www.bushwoodbooks.co.uk

I dedicate this tale to my fellow travelers through Mouse's backyard…
Joy Scott and Mark Bee.

Observing with New Eyes

A White-footed Mouse's territory measures around a fifth of an acre, or the equivalent of a backyard measuring 30 × 25 meters (100 × 80 feet), an area that is inhabited by a colorful and diverse group of creatures. Even in the tiny space of a small mouse's backyard, natural wonders occur on leaves, under logs, in the soil—just about everywhere, if we look closely and carefully. The details of the different scenes from Mouse's backyard emphasize the complexity of even these smallest habitats. We do not have to travel to distant jungles, mountains, or seashores to experience the pleasures that nature offers everywhere. Every square foot of a forest, a meadow, a schoolyard, or a backyard can be rich with life and energy. Be patient, observe carefully; and beautiful, hidden worlds will unfold. Wherever we venture, patience and careful observation offer rich rewards.

As we follow the paths in Mouse's backyard, an appreciation of the landscape that is so familiar to Mouse and his neighbors unfolds. We begin wondering and caring about this new and unknown world, asking questions about what life is like for the inhabitants of this small world.

Close, microscopic encounters with these creatures reveal hidden worlds within the small world that Mouse calls home. What we discover from microscopic examination of the creatures encountered in Mouse's backyard is that a common plan underlies the great diversity in shapes and sizes of life on earth—from microbes to whales. All creatures share cells as their building blocks. We all are made up of one or more of these cells. And it is these cells that can arrange into countless, lovely combinations—such as flowers, leaves, eyes, and wings—and into countless creatures—such as snails, trees, fungi, and butterflies. Close encounters in Mouse's backyard instill not only an appreciation of the worth of even the smallest creatures that live there, but also a scientific understanding of those features that impart life to all these creatures. As Roman Vishniac observed, "In nature every bit of life is lovely. And the more magnification we use, the more details are brought out, perfectly formed, like endless sets of boxes within boxes."

This exploration of Mouse's backyard has been documented in drawings, photographs, and verse. Two talented companions accompanied me on this expedition. Mark Bee has an appreciation for the beauty and intricacy of microscopic life that he has captured in his unparalleled photographs. Joy Scott has been a patient listener to my ideas, a careful reader of my words, and a source of so many good suggestions. As I wrote and rewrote, she read and reread until the verses that relate our discoveries flowed smoothly over the tongue and the ear. As each drawing emerged from its page, Joy was able to stand back and see where and how its many parts could be manipulated to convey the most appeal and most information.

Michael Jeffords is well known as a nature photographer whose images reflect the eye of an artist, the heart of a naturalist, and the mind of a scientist. Scenes from his photographs helped guide the preparation of many drawings; Michael provided all these photographs with his characteristic generosity.

We thank the Beckman Institute at the University of Illinois for providing the electron microscope that has transported us to many of these hidden worlds. The magnifications of these hidden worlds are expressed as either a fraction or a multiple of the thickness of a nickel (2mm = about 1/12 inch) or the width of one of our hairs (1/10 mm = about 1/250 inch).

The great opportunity is where you are. Do not despise your own place and hour. Every place is under the stars, every place is the center of the world.

–John Burroughs

Contents

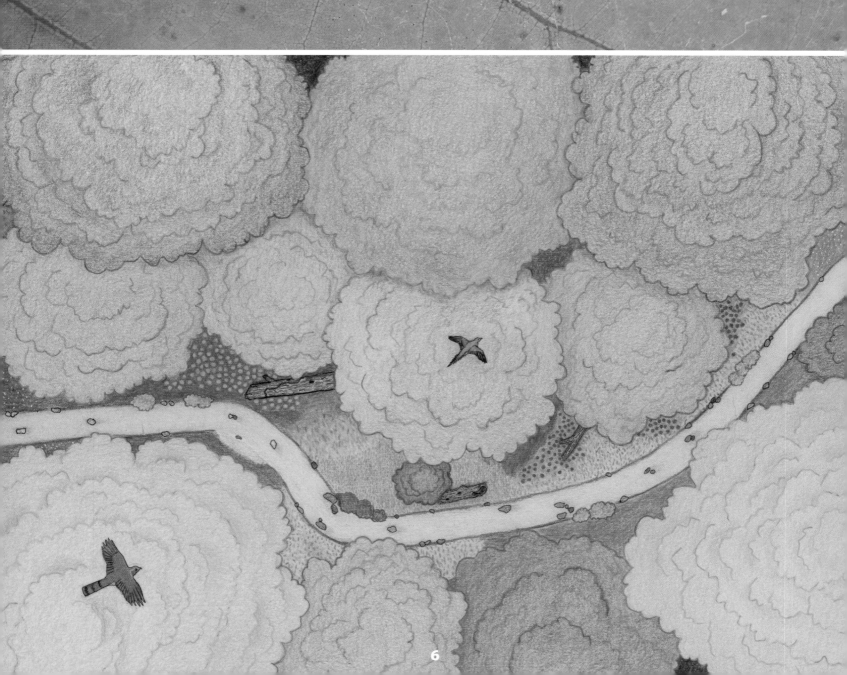

A mouse's yard is not very long or very wide,
But it is amazing what you can find inside.
So many different creatures live in the yard
That naming them would be extremely hard.

From the sky high above,
As viewed by a hawk or a dove,
Mouse's yard is a quiet, wooded spot;
But dull and uneventful, it certainly is not.

Mouse had learned to avoid every hawk—
Never to loiter and never to gawk.
He cautiously peeked from a hole in the log,
Where he peacefully lived with a gray tree frog.

As Hawk gazed down on the log below,
There was no way for her to know
That a mouse and a frog lived happily there,
In the beautiful woods with its fresh, clean air.

Hawk

With eyes that act like telescopes, it is true
That hawk eyes magnify more than most eyes do.
Hawks can spot creatures farther away
Than the eyes of humans or mice any day.
Eye cells capture light and pass images to brains.
Cone cells capture light and the colors it contains.
Bird eyes have many cone cells; our eyes have few.
Birds see a sharper, more colorful world than we do.

A slice through a mouse's eye from front to back (Shutterstock Images)

Eye to eye with a mouse (Rob & Ann Simpson, Visuals Unlimited)

Eye to eye with a hawk (David L. Ross Jr.)

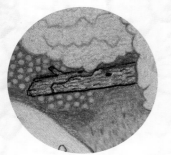

A patch of earth

Of creatures there is no dearth,
That can be found in a fistful of earth.
Of creatures that inhabit a single tree,
There are far more than our eyes can see.

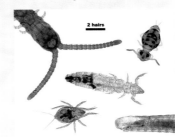

2 hairs

A few of the many creatures that live in a fistful of earth

Dove

From Dove's wing, a feather drifted down.
Mouse watched as it twirled around.
It landed gently by a shaggy grape vine,
Where Mouse admired its intricate design.

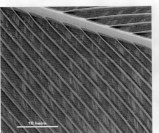

10 hairs

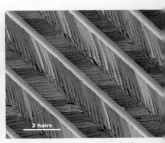

2 hairs

A close-up view of a dove's feather

An even closer view of a dove's feather

Awakening of the Woods

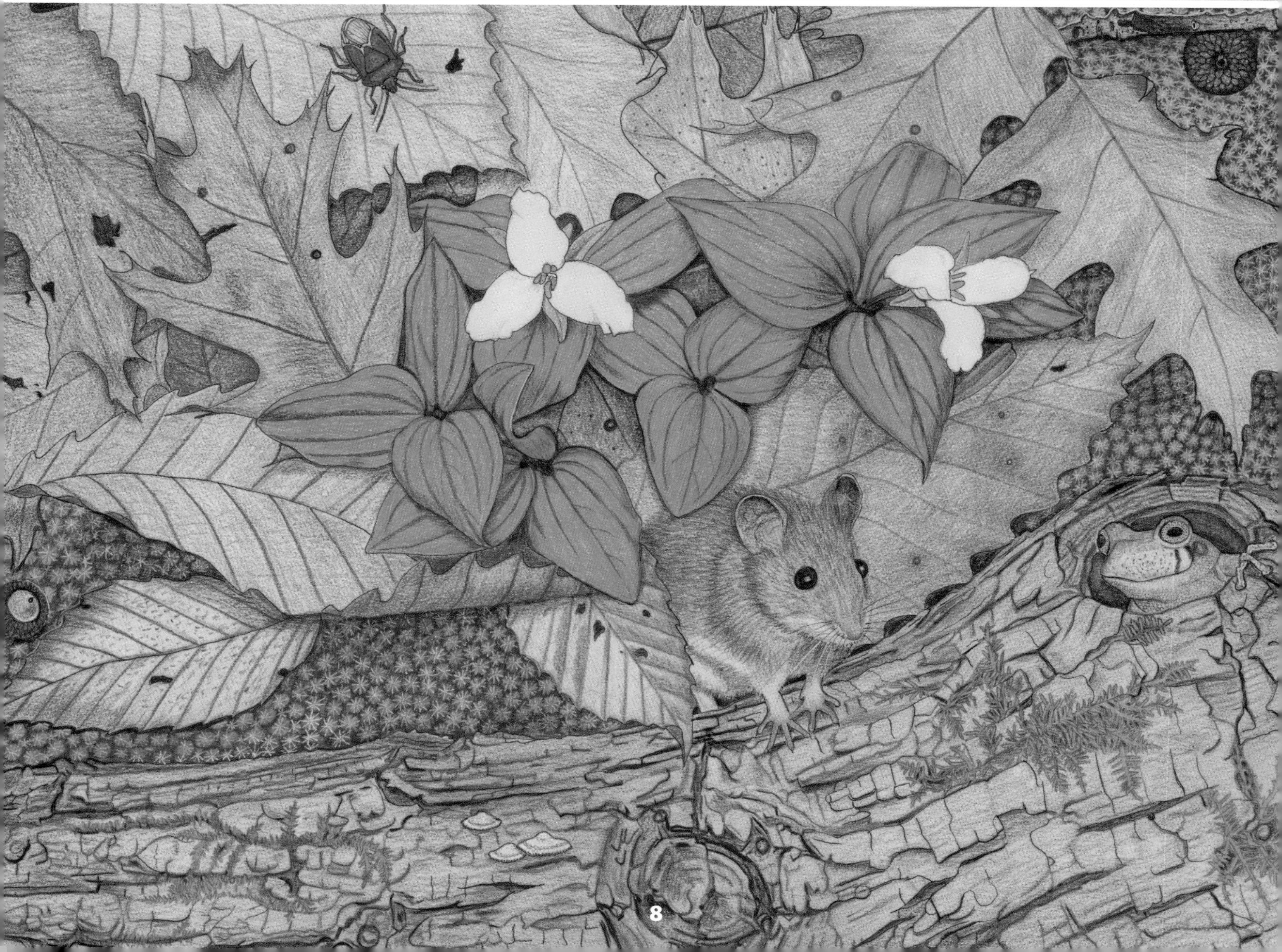

Mouse had had enough of ice and snow,
And at last he felt a warm wind blow.
Mouse was now eager to explore
Places he had never seen before.

He sniffed, pawed, and chewed as well;
And soon he began to see and smell
A world under his whiskers and his paw
That awakened his curiosity and his awe.

Mouse loved to explore for hours
And often stopped to sniff the flowers.
Mouse was soon able to tell
Every flower's special smell.

Frog, however, was a sleepy head;
She just loved to lie in bed.
But when she heard sounds of spring,
Frog was inspired to rise and sing.

Stink Bug

Stink Bug had slept under leaves beneath the snow.
She now gladly left her leafy bed below.
Spreading her green wings she began her first trip
In search of green shoots whose sap she could sip.
With a long, straight beak that acts like a straw,
She impales a shoot whose sap she'll withdraw.

Stink Bug's long beak lies on its belly.

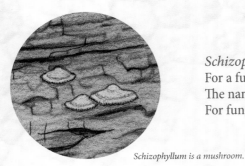

Schizophyllum is a mushroom.

Schizophyllum is a name—rather long but good—
For a fuzzy mushroom that sprouts from wood.
The name *schizo*, or split, certainly seems fit
For fungal gills, or *phylla*, that are hairy and split.

The hairy and split gills of Schizophyllum

Snow Trillium

The snow trilliums were all blooming,
As warm days of spring were looming.
Snow trilliums were first to appear on the forest floor,
Followed by Spring Beauty, Trout Lily, and many more.
Trilliums each with three leaves sprout and start,
Adding three or two times three of each flower part.
It is easy to see why *tri*, meaning three,
Is part of the name for this flower you see.

Looking into a trillium flower

Beetles in the Backyard

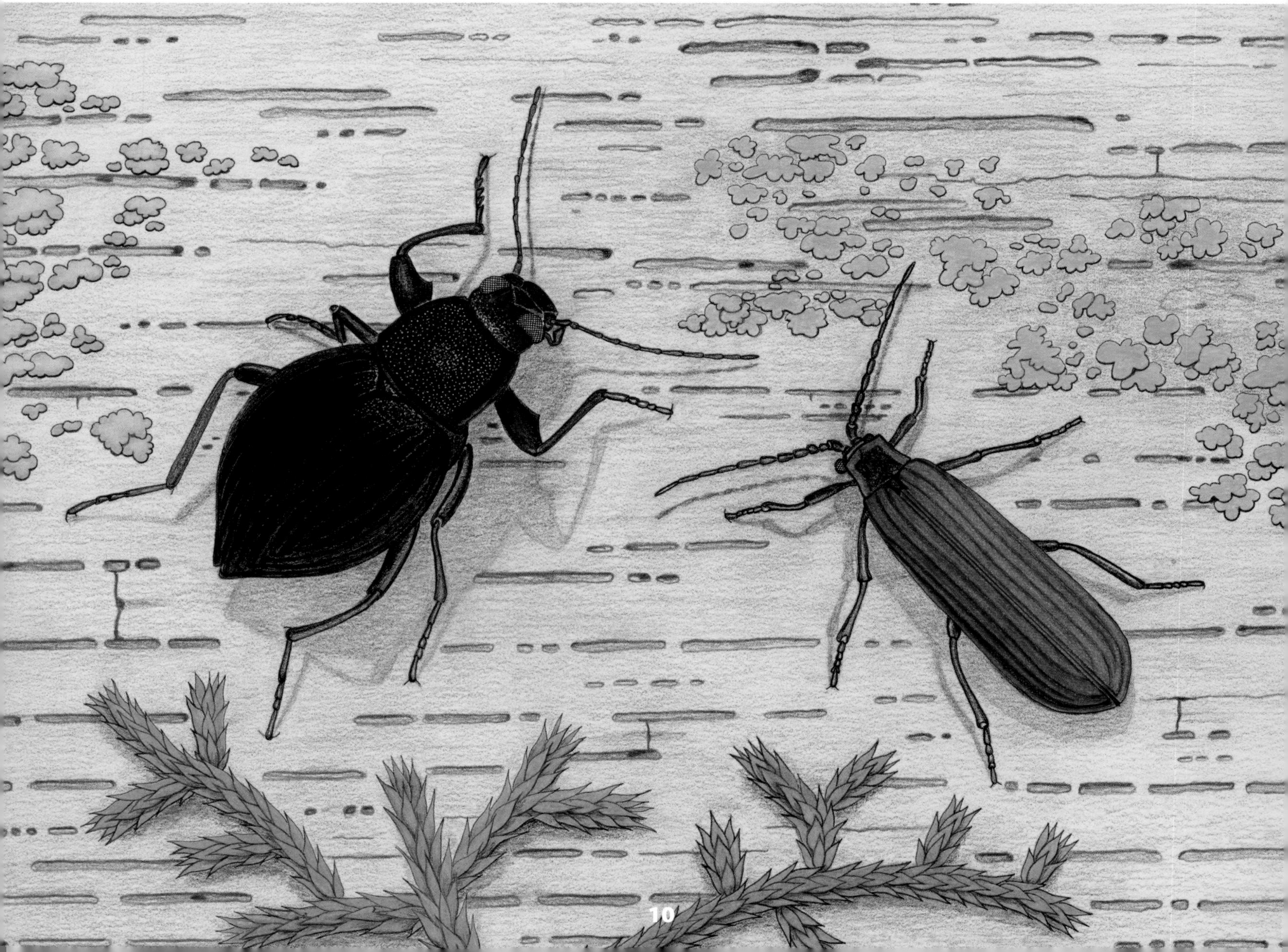

In Mouse's yard, beetles live everywhere—
In the stream, in the ground, in the air.
Across the log thousands of beetle feet tromp;
And in the log's dark tunnels, beetle larvae chomp.

Two beetles met in the log's lichen bed,
One dark black and one bright red.
In the log, they had grown up only inches away
But had never met until this day.

Beetles can love; beetles can fly.
On a keen sense of smell they have come to rely.
Beetles can feel; beetles can chew.
All these things beetles can do.

A Lichen is an unusual mosaic creature—
Part fungus, part alga is its special feature.
Fungus and alga live and work as one.
Together they get Lichen's job done.

Lichen on the log

Lichens come in many hues—
Reds, greens, yellows, even blues.
Lichens grow on rocks, logs, and bark.
Lichens love light and shun the dark.
If we cut through the lichens as we slice bread,
We see round cells and some shaped like thread.
These algal cells and fungal threads, we could say,
Look like a plate of olives and spaghetti sliced this way.

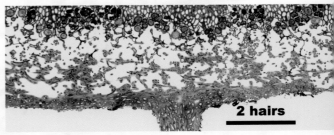

2 hairs

A slice of lichen

Red Beetle

Hard wing covers are found on all beetles' backs.
Each is sculpted with ridges, grooves, and tracks.
Its many bristles and hairs are sensitive to touch,
And about its environment, tell a beetle very much.

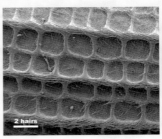

2 hairs

A close look at Red Beetle's back

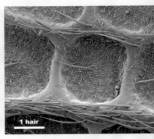

1 hair

An even closer look at Red Beetle's back

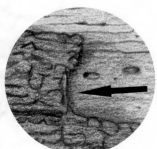

Beneath the bark of the log

Some beetles are flat, fierce and live under bark,
Where they pounce on other creatures in the dark.
Other beetles are round, retiring, and slow.
They peacefully graze wherever fungi grow.

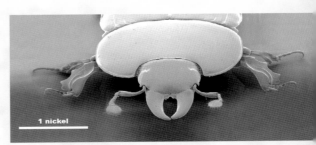

1 nickel

This fierce, flat beetle lives under bark.

Mouse meandered through the geranium bed
And then began to cross the fallen branch ahead.
He abruptly came face to face with Snail
Who happened to be crossing Mouse's trail.

The scent of wild geraniums filled the air,
And insects came from everywhere.
Along the border of this flower patch,
Frog ate flies that were so easy to catch.

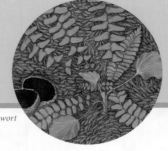

Devil's Urn and Ebony Spleenwort

Click Beetle

Click Beetle stumbled on a crack,
Falling from the log onto her back.
She landed upside down on mossy ground;
But with a swift "click," she flipped around.

A fern named Ebony Spleenwort
Is a sensitive and elegant sort.
With tiny leaflets and dark brown stalk,
It grows where snails crawl and ants walk.
And in the shadow of this lovely fern,
Grows a mushroom called Devil's Urn.

Snail

Snail is a creature that creeps, not walks,
And that looks about with eyes on stalks.
Across leaves and logs it moves on its belly,
Leaving a trail that is sticky like jelly.

Snail's eyes are perched on stalks.

Flower of Wild Geranium

Hidden hairs of a flower confer
The secret of each flower's allure.
These hairs produce nectar, tasty and sweet,
Attracting bees, beetles, flies to their treat.

Looking into the center of the flower

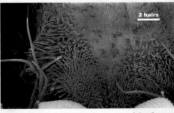

Looking even closer into the center of the flower

Red Velvet Mite's toe

Face to face with Red Velvet Mite

Velvet Mite

Velvet Mite is often met as it scurries about,
Hunting tiny prey along a familiar mossy route.
It is covered with long hairs and is crimson red
From the tips of its claws to the top of its head.

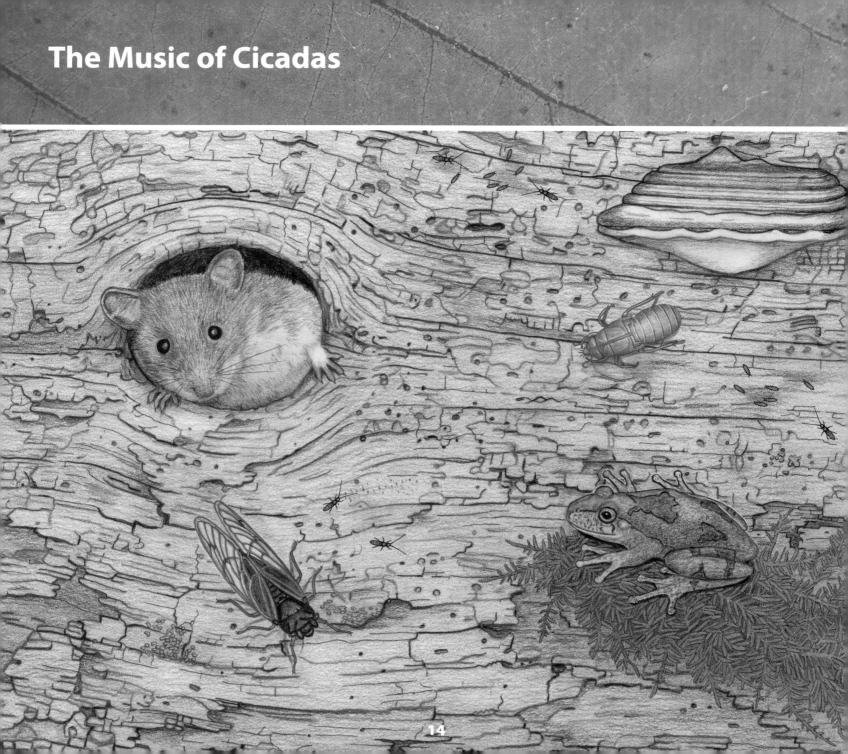

Mouse awoke to an awful roar
That echoed from treetops to forest floor.
This was a sound that had not been heard
By any living mouse, frog, or bird.

Only once in his life will Mouse hear such a sound,
When cicadas leave their homes beneath the ground.
Millions that had fed seventeen years from spring to fall,
Shed their skins, spread their wings, and begin to call.

Mouse found it hard to decide
If he should take a peek outside.
Frog's trill was soothing to his ears
And helped calm his many fears.

Where Cicada's ears are found

Mice have ears that twitch and turn to pick up sound.
On frogs and cicadas only flat eardrums are found.
These eardrums vibrate to sound waves in the air,
And touch tiny hairs on nerve cells found there.
As vibrations pass to the hairs these cells contain,
The signal from hairs becomes sound in the brain.

Frog's ear

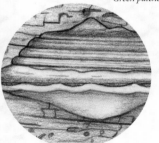

Green patches and Springtails

Green patches on logs and bark of trees
Survive summer heat and winter freeze.
The patches become green pastures on days
When tiny Springtails come out to graze.
Green patches contain plants so small
That they have no roots or leaves at all.

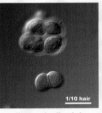

Small, round cells of algae make up the green patches on the log.

Springtail's face

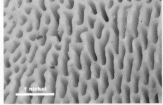

Shelf Mushroom

Frog gazed up at the pattern of mushroom pores
From which Mushroom had shed so many spores.
Mushroom gave Frog a porch from rain and sun,
And a place to perch when each day was done.

Mushroom pores are found on Mushroom's lower surface.

Close-up of Mushroom spores found inside Mushroom pores.

After leaving the underground, Cicada sheds this skin of its nymph and spreads its wings.

Cicadas have big claws and fearsome faces.
All the years they live in underground places.
When each is finally ready to shed its skin,
Its new adventures aboveground can begin.

Face, claws, and beak of a Cicada nymph

15

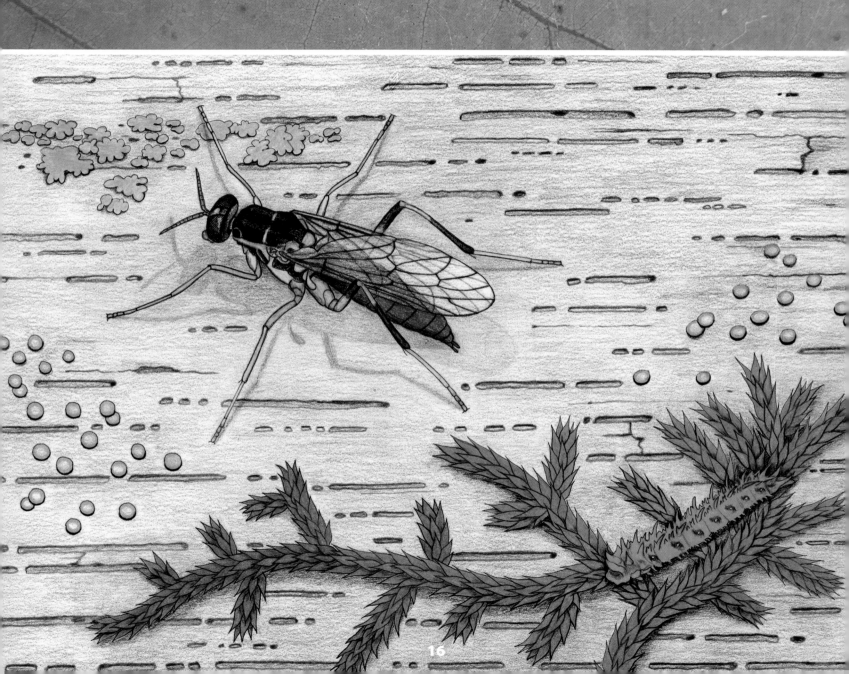

1 hair

The birth of a moss is too amazing to ignore,
When a thread of green cells sprouts from a spore,
And soon gives rise to leaves, rootlets, and more.
This first green thread accounts for the name
That each baby moss or protonema can claim.
Combining the words *proto,* for first, *nema,* for thread,
Forms not an English name, but a Greek one instead.

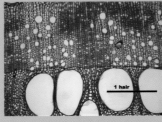
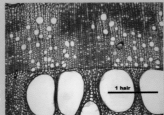

Many cells large and small make up oak wood.

1 hair

Fungi and insects had worked away at its wood
Until only an outer shell of the old log still stood.
The beauty of the old oak wood is concealed
Until its cells with a microscope are revealed.

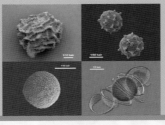

Clockwise from top left: A Christmas fern spore, two mushroom spores, a horsetail spore with its four coiled elaters, and a moss spore

Each spore has inside it what it will take,
A complete mushroom or plant to make.
Spores of mushrooms, mosses, ferns, horsetails
Are tiny packets filled with countless details.
On a period of this page, many spores can sit.
From 10 to 150 spores can side by side fit.

Liogma is the larva of a fly;
And on moss, it has come to rely.
With its shape and color it achieves
Flawless camouflage among the leaves.

Liogma

Xylomyid does not seem such an unusual name
Once you understand from whence it came.
The Greek "*xylo*" for wood and "*myid*" for fly
Tell us where these insects live, grow, and die.

Xylomyid Fly

Mosses, like trees, have leaves and shoots,
But not long roots or even ripe fruits.
Each moss, like a fern, arises from just one spore,
Without flower, seed, or anything more.

Moss leaves and shoots

On top of logs, tiny mushrooms stand out
And arise as hidden fungi grow and sprout.
Cells of fungi are arranged in chains
That lie within dark and hidden lanes.
Without a mouth or a gut, fungi readily eat
All the decaying wood that they meet.

Tiny Mushrooms

In the Horsetail Forest

Damselfly among the Horsetails

Mayfly among the Horsetails

Mouse and Frog climbed among horsetails
In a forest where there were few if any trails.
Mayfly and Damselfly fluttered by
Among plants measuring over ten-mice high.

On this very spot, ages before Mouse passed by,
There grew horsetails that were three hundred-mice high.
Giant ancestors of insects also flew through the air
In the ancient coal forests that grew and thrived there.

Earth Tongue Mushrooms

Mouse spotted beetles he had never seen before,
As they ambled over fallen leaves of sycamore.
One beetle was blue; one beetle was brown.
One had antennae that were fluffy like down.

Mushrooms with strange forms had sprouted below,
Where bright yellow Earth Tongues stretch and grow.
And round Puffballs are filled with countless spores
That rise like clouds from their wide-open pores.

Blue Beetle

Brown Beetle

Puffballs

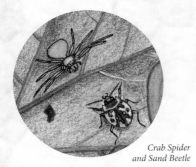

Ptilodactylid Beetle

Ptilodactylid is an awfully long name
For such a small, brown beetle to claim.
Ptilo translates as wing; *dactyl* translates as toe,
As anyone familiar with Greek would know.
Its antennae, feathery and long, act like a nose
And are far more noticeable than its tiny toes.

Portrait of Ptilodactylid Beetle

Crab Spider and Sand Beetle

Crab Spider quickly scooted to the right,
When Sand Beetle appeared in her sight.
She spread her eight legs in alarm,
Even though Sand Beetle meant no harm.

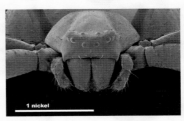

Crab spider looks at us with eight eyes.

Horsetail stems

Having sandy grains in its stem, as they all do,
Makes each horsetail especially tough to chew.
A horsetail has no tasty parts or even a flower,
But pioneers used its stems to scrub and scour.
Leaves breathe through many pores
That open and shut just like doors.
Stoma, or mouth, is the name for a single pore;
Stomata, or mouths, is the name for two or more.
Since leaves on horsetails are never found,
Their stems have *stomata* arrayed all around.

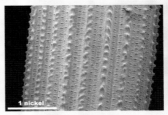

A horsetail stem has its stomata arranged in neat rows.

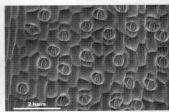

A leaf from a nearby flower has stomata that are scattered about.

Mouse did not believe in logs being haunted,
As he entered through the hole undaunted.
But when he saw a bat across the way,
He began to doubt his courage that day.

Mouse thought Bat was a strange mouse
That hung upside down in its log house.
Bat thought Mouse was a very strange bat
That had no wings and walked like a rat.

Bat was tired after a long flight,
And was also startled by this sight.
He gazed down at a frightened Mouse
That had crossed the threshold of his house.

Mouse saw that Frog was calm and bright,
And was soon comforted by that sight.
To Mouse a wise saying soon became clear,
That, "To understand is better than to fear."

Cobweb Spider

Seeing a large, busy spider overhead
Did nothing to ease Mouse's dread.
In its silken web were two flies and a gnat,
And Mouse was upset by the sight of that.
Spider's spinnerets spun the silk, long and fine,
That trapped the insects on which it would dine.

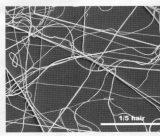

Cobweb Spider has five spinnerets at the tip its abdomen.

Fine, tangled silk spun from Spider's spinnerets.

Bat

Bat was hanging upside down,
And his fur was soft and brown.
Each of his hairs was thin and fine,
Much thinner than yours or mine.
Over the treetops, Bat could fly—
Something Mouse dared not try.

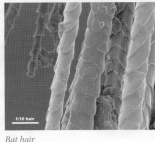

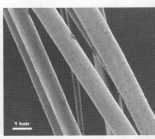

Bat hair

Human hair

Bats snatch flying insects from the air—
Flies, mosquitoes, gnats, and similar fare.
Each insect has a crunchy outer shell
That each bat must crush and chew well.
A bat dropping is a jigsaw puzzle of insect remains;
Wings, legs, and other crunchy parts it contains.

Many different insect parts are found in Bat's dropping.

At the Water Hole

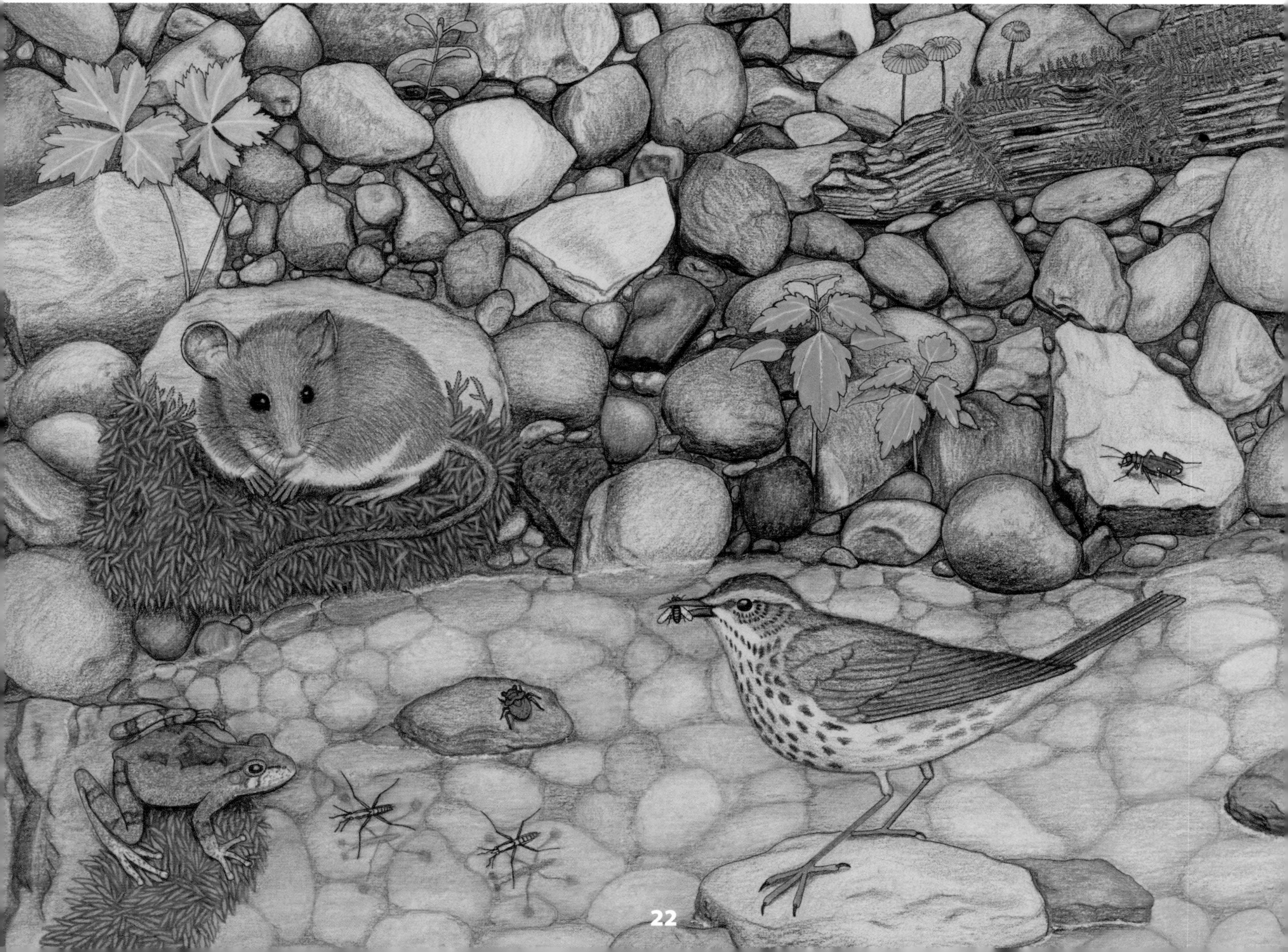

Mouse came to the water hole of the creek each day,
Clambering over rocks of many colors on the way.
On a favorite rock he settled, where soft moss grew,
And from there he always encountered something new.

Mouse gazed across the way at a bird
That sang one of the loveliest songs he had heard.
The bird wagged its tail as it perched by the creek,
Obviously pleased to have snatched a fly in its beak.

Frog gazed from her rock, mossy and green,
At the strangest toad she had ever seen.
Like a toad it had warts, as many or more.
It could hop like a toad but had six legs, not four.

Tiger Beetle

With jaws like sickles and with sharp eyesight,
Tiger Beetle hunts stream banks in bright sunlight.
Her movements are all swift and bold,
And her emerald green is stunning to behold.

Tiger Beetle's face

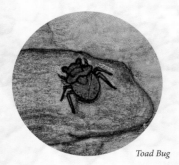

Toad Bug

Toad bugs are hunters on the banks of the creek.
They pounce on the smaller insects they seek.
With sharp beak, each bug has mastered a way
Of impaling and draining the blood of its prey.
They actually blend so well with rocks on the shore
That they are hard to see until they pounce once more.

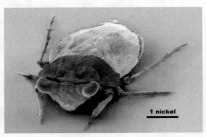

Toad Bug has "buggy" eyes and a warty complexion.

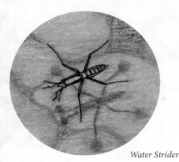

Water Strider

Water Striders can walk on water in the stream.
For Mouse and Frog such talent is only a dream.
While hairs that repel water keep each toe dry,
On the two claws of each toe, striders also rely.
At the water's surface only claws pierce and grip,
Providing the traction for each strider's trip.
Dimples on the water form around each toe
And cast round shadows on the rocks below.

Water Strider's hairy toe

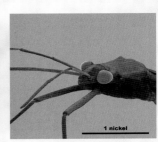

Water Strider has large eyes, a long beak, and very long legs.

Foxfire and Fireflies

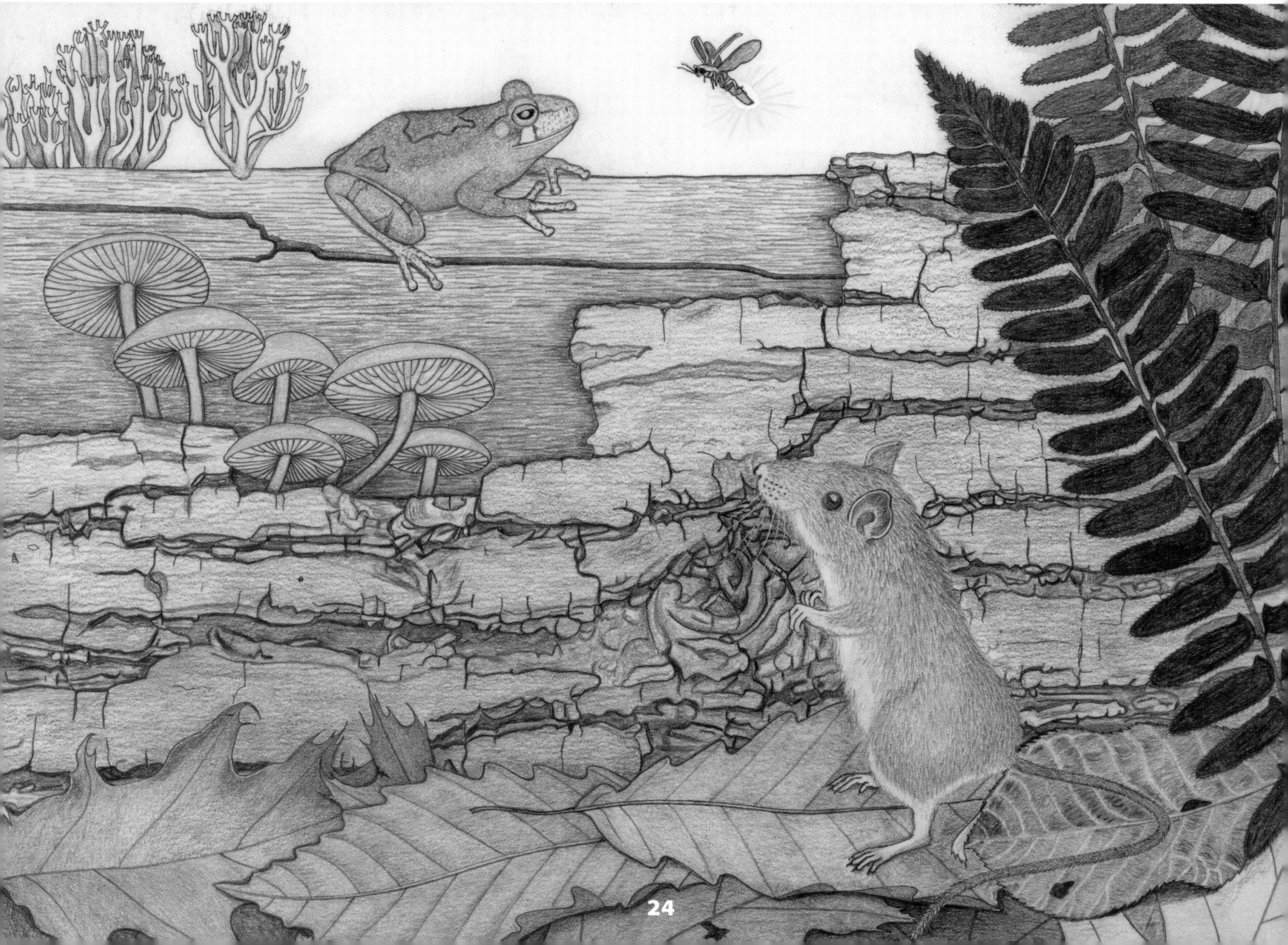

Mushrooms are remarkable creatures
With some truly exceptional features.
Some grow on wood and bark.
Some even glow in the dark.

Coral Mushrooms look like corals from the sea,
With beautiful colors and with branches like a tree.
Other mushrooms glow with a soft light
And on dark nights produce an eerie sight.

Coral Mushrooms

Foxfire is the name given to a mushroom's glow.
Very few have seen its unforgettable show.
Even Mouse rose and stood in awe
At the glowing mushrooms that he saw.

Firefly's lamp produces its own glow
That sheds light above, around, and below
So other fireflies nearby can see
How bright and flashy Firefly can be.

Mushrooms that glow

Mushrooms form when fungi leave the dark and fruit,
As threads of fungi assemble and send forth a shoot.
A section through a single stalk and gills reveals
The tiny threads and spores that its cap conceals.

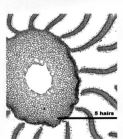

A slice through Mushroom's cap shows stalk, gills, threads, and spores.

A closer look at Mushroom's cap

Firefly

The cells of Firefly's lamp are large and round.
Within them, compounds that light up are found.
Energy from Firefly's food gets them all to unite.
When they fall apart, this energy transforms to light.
For saving energy, firefly lamps cannot be beat,
Since firefly lamps lose almost no energy as heat.

A slice through Firefly's lamp reveals lamp cells that flash and glow. Two of these cells have been colored yellow to stand out from their fellow lamp cells.

Christmas Fern

Although Christmas Fern is green all year,
June is the time when Fern's spores appear.
Look under its leaves and you will see
Many packets where spores happen to be.
What look like tiny parasols shelter them there,
As spores drop from their packets into the air.

Fern spores are found on the under side of Fern's leaf.

On the old log a mushroom garden grew.
Among the moss a fern had sprouted too.
Creatures visit the garden from far and near
To enjoy the sights and smells they find here.

Mouse was crossing new territory today,
As he scaled the old log that lay in his way.
This log was having a remarkable rebirth,
As it slowly returned to a welcoming earth.

*A fern among
the moss*

Frog found insects to her liking,
As she and Mouse went hiking.
Her tongue snatched insects from the air
And from all the fungi growing there.

Stilt-legged flies
Have lovely red eyes.
In mushroom gardens they are mostly found,
Where on spindly legs they prance around.

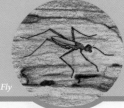

Stilt-legged Fly

Millipede

Millipedes accomplish quite a feat in coordinating all their feet.
And watching their many legs move in waves is quite a treat.
They move across leaves and rocks, over and under logs,
Always keeping a safe distance from hungry frogs.
But for Frog, tasting one millipede is more than enough,
For millipedes produce some awful, distasteful stuff.

*Pouches (see arrows) on
Millipede's sides produce and
expel awfully distasteful stuff.*

*Two moss stalks
and their capsules
rise above the
moss leaves.*

Above Moss's leaves, spore stalks stand tall.
From their capsules, spores scatter, spores fall.
Into a green moss, each spore germinates;
And as a daughter or a son, each culminates. ·
The moss life cycle will again be complete,
When mother moss and father moss meet.
After their meeting, a new spore stalk will sprout;
And from its capsule, spores again will shower out.

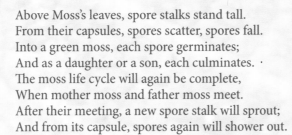

*Each moss capsule is filled
with spores and perches
on a stalk high above the
moss leaves.*

*A close-up of a moss capsule
filled with spores.*

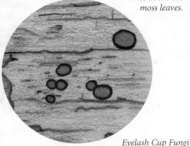

Eyelash Cup Fungi

Spores had sprouted in the mushroom bed
Into fungi that are bright orange and red.
These dark lashes, straight and long,
To the Eyelash Cup Fungus belong.

*Fern spores are found on the
under side of Fern's leaf.*

Over the oak log and through fallen leaves,
Daddy Longlegs waddles and weaves.
Waving his legs to and fro through the air
Helps him decide who and what are where.

Mouse was dreaming about a beetle lunch,
As he recalled how they taste and crunch.
Beetles with mushrooms was a favorite treat,
Followed by all the beechnuts he could eat.

Fungus Beetle can smell mushrooms from far away.
Mushrooms provide her home and meals each day.
Her orange and her black are shiny and bright
And are such a conspicuous, appealing sight.
Hungry Frog and Mouse usually look twice
Until they learn that her taste is not at all nice.

Frog had watched many travelers pass today,
As each of them hurried on its way.
Some with six legs; some with four;
Some with eight legs; some with more.

Fungus Beetle

*Daddy Longlegs as
viewed from his side*

Over leaves Daddy Longlegs steps with care,
Watching for dangers that might lurk there.
He surveys the landscape far and nigh
With his periscopic eyes poised high.

*Daddy Longlegs as viewed
from above*

*Face to face with Daddy
Longlegs, whose two eyes are
perched on top of its body.*

Pseudoscorpion

Pseudoscorpion usually lies hidden in dark
Until she decides to climb a leaf and embark.
When Daddy Longlegs passes her way,
She hitches a ride aboard without delay,
Journeying to new places that very day.

*Tiny Pseudoscorpion has
big claws and big jaws.*

*Beneath
fallen leaves*

Beneath fallen leaves countless creatures toil,
Transforming leaves and returning them to soil.
With very little, microbes do a great deal,
And they do so with much talent and zeal.
"Small is beautiful" seems obvious and true
Once you see what microbes are able to do.
They are the most abundant creatures for sure.
Without them, no other life would endure.
Microbes transform, recycle, and renew.
No other creatures can do all that they do.

*Decaying leaves are covered by bacteria
and threads of fungi. Cells of different
bacteria have been colored to stand out
against the surface of the decaying leaf.*

*A mite ventures across a
leaf and through a forest
of fungal threads.*

Acorns from oak trees are falling all around,
And *thump, thump, thump* as they strike the ground.
To the ears of mice, chipmunks, squirrels, and jays,
Few sounds are so welcome on these autumn days.

Fungi help return leaves and logs to soil
And do so with little obvious effort and toil.
They have wood and leaves for breakfast and lunch
And silently digest their food without even a crunch.

Acorns from a red oak and a chinkapin oak lie next to hickory nuts that Mouse has already opened.

A colorful mushroom called Turkey-Tail
Has many stripes, some bright, some pale.
Under the bark of the log it grows and spreads,
Recycling the wood with its long fungal threads.

Turkey-Tail Mushroom

Auricularia is a mushroom that looks like an ear,
But it has never acquired the ability to hear.
It grows on wood and is soft, rubbery, and brown,
Tasty food for beetles, mice, even people in town.

Auricularia, the Ear Mushroom

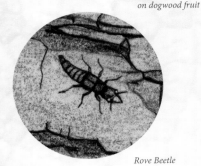

Mouse munching on dogwood fruit

Red fruits of the dogwood tree
Are filled with food and energy.
Each fruit cell has round droplets of fat.
Few fruits have more energy than that.
Fats nourish birds for long autumn flights,
And prepare mice for cold winter nights.

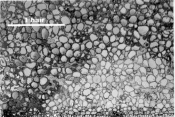

A slice through a dogwood fruit reveals cells filled with round droplets of energy-rich fat.

Rove Beetle

Prowling along mushrooms stalks and among their gills,
Rove Beetle intently hunts for his insect meals.
With jaws like sickles, he catches and eats his prey.
He is so voracious he devours many each day.

Rove Beetle hunting for a meal.

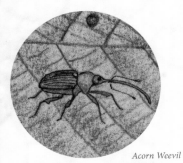

Acorn Weevil

Acorn Weevil has a long, curved snout.
Tiny jaws at its very tip do not look too stout.
But into an acorn, mother Weevil's jaws did chew;
And here her eggs hatched and her larvae grew.

Meeting Acorn Weevil face to face

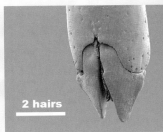

The jaws at the very tip of Acorn Weevil's long snout.

Frog and Mouse gazed up in awe
At all the colorful leaves they saw.
Bright and stunning were the colors of each,
From maple and oak, sassafras, and beech.

An autumn leaf drifted down
From a faraway tree's crown.
Its colors of red, orange, and gold
Were really a pleasure to behold.

In many colors and forms, mushrooms sprout;
And some unusual ones certainly stand out.
Gnarled and black, as they reach for the light,
Dead Man's Fingers are a strange, eerie sight.

Dead Man's Fingers

Apron mosses provide homes that please
The hidden creatures on trunks of trees.
Here the creatures remain unseen,
Where these mosses drape their green.

Apron Moss

Maple leaf

This maple leaf had once been dark green.
Now inside its cells other colors are seen.
As the green fades, these colors just glow,
Decorating the forest before the first snow.

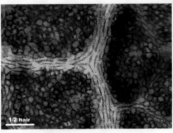

*Cells of leaves lose their green color of
summer and take on new colors of autumn.*

Bird's Nest Fungi

Bird's Nest Fungus is filled with "eggs" that fly
When drops of rain propel them far and high.
An "egg" is made of many threads and spores.
When it lands, it "hatches," grows and explores.

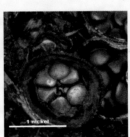

Bird's Nest Fungi

*A closer look at an "egg"
from Bird's Nest Fungus*

Lacewing

With golden eyes and gossamer wings,
Lacewings look like such delicate things.
But they are hardy insects for sure
That winter's cold months can endure.
By producing antifreeze as winter arrives,
Each lacewing among fallen leaves survives.

A portrait of Lacewing

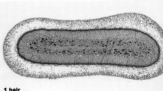

*A slice through an "egg"
from Bird's Nest Fungus*

34

Stoneflies dance upon the snow,
As Mouse and Junco watch their show.
Some Stoneflies land on top the log, some land below,
Wherever their favorite lichens, moss, and fungi grow.
Other insects prefer warm days and bright flowers,
But Winter Stoneflies are out in snow and cold for hours.

Winter Stoneflies

Earthstar sheds its countless spores
Over the mosses on forest floors.
While distant stars set the heavens aglow,
Earthstars brighten the ground below.

Earthstar Mushroom

Mushrooms are also out and about.
Their colors and shapes really stand out.
Witches' Butter looks like lemon jello.
It is such a bright and glossy yellow.

Witches' Butter Mushroom

In a few weeks Junco will prepare to depart
For a forest where a new family she will start.
There in the North Woods she will nest and stay
Until short days of autumn send her back our way.

Junco

The apothecia of lichens, tiny cups resemble,
Where inside thousands of spores assemble.
An apothecium is like an apothecary
As we learn from any Greek dictionary.
Apothecaries are places known as drugstores,
While apothecia are places for fungal spores.

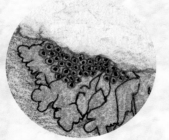

Apothecia of Lichen

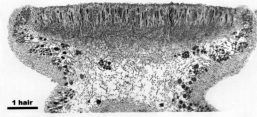

A slice through the many spores, fungal threads, and round algal cells of an apothecium

On spring days when oak leaves are starting to grow,
Wasps emerge from galls on the dead leaves below.
Each wasp lays an egg on a leaf, still tender and small,
A portion of which will expand and transform to a gall.
The creation of an oak gall is a remarkable feat,
When a tiny Gall Wasp and a growing leaf meet.
Galls can be spiny, bumpy, or round,
And many other forms also abound.

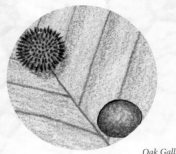

Oak Galls

A round and bumpy gall on an oak leaf

That mosses and liverworts are related,
Among biologists is no longer debated.
These tiny plants stay green all year round,
Whether growing on trees or over the ground.
Each cell in their leaves has packets of green
That under a microscope can be readily seen.

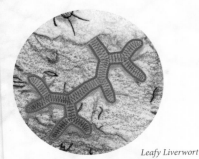

Leafy Liverwort

Each leaf of Leafy Liverwort is made of many green cells.

A closer look at green cells in a leaf of Leafy Liverwort

The End of a Long Winter

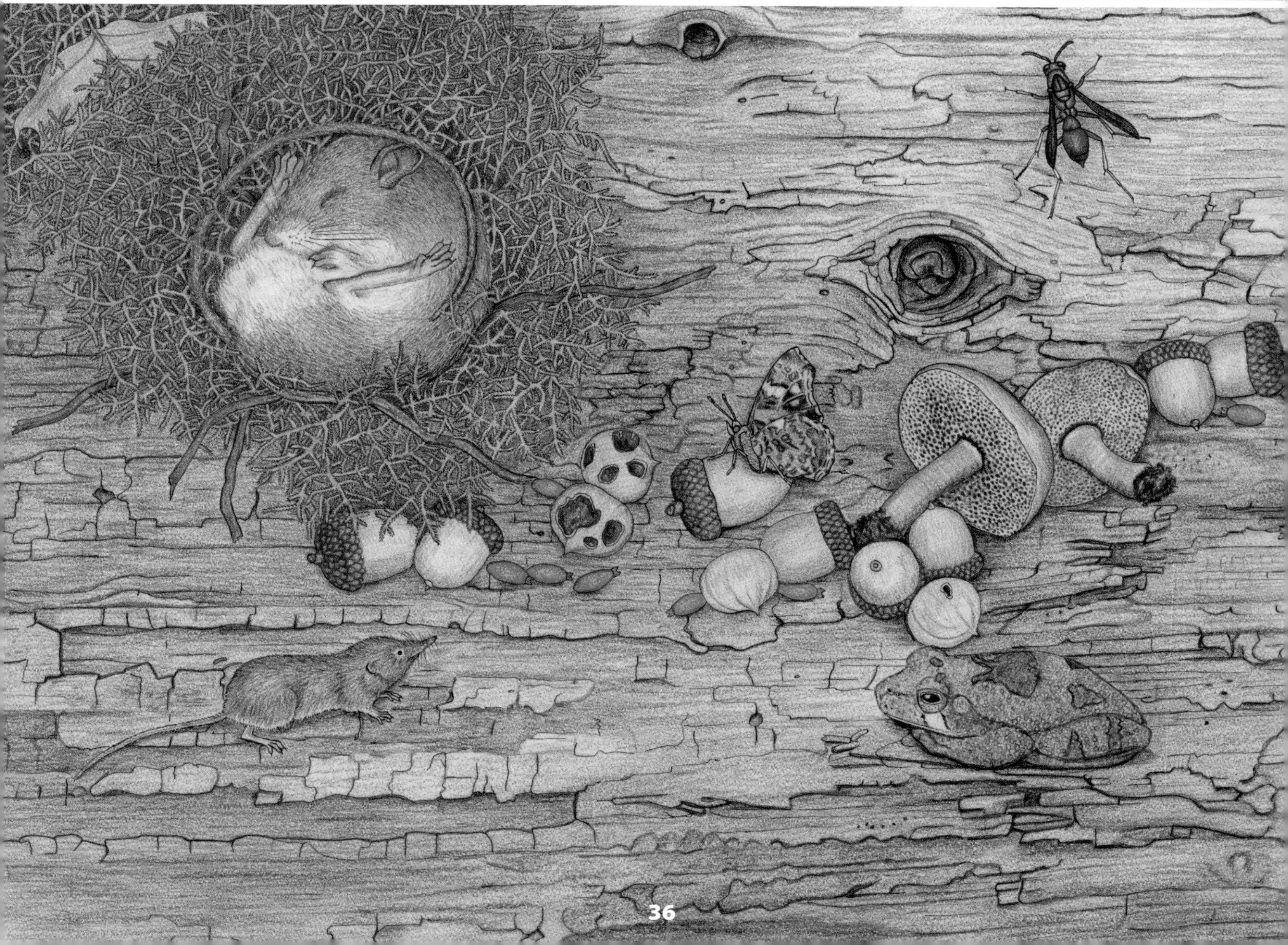

On a bed of moss, Mouse fell sound asleep.
Frog was so tired; she uttered not a peep.
Only Shrew was busy as shrews always are,
Sniffing and checking the log near and far.

Before settling down for his long winter sleep,
Mouse had stored mushrooms and nuts, many acorns deep.
How good the food tasted on a cold winter day,
And how cozy and warm was the bed where he lay.
The old log welcomed all from the wet and cold—
Whether they were small or large, timid or bold.

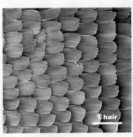

Shrew

Mouse's nose twitched with delight
As it picked up a lovely smell one night.
It was the scent of a flower he knew,
Carried by the air as a warm wind blew.

As Mouse stretched and prepared to depart,
Even sleepy Frog arose with a start.
The smells, songs, and warmth in the air
Made both of them happy just to be there.

In the log where Mouse and Frog were tucked away,
Wasp and Butterfly had found a place to stay,
Through many blizzards and winter nights,
Until birds began their long northern flights.
Butterfly's wings impart bright colors to spring.
Their many scales overlap and cover each wing.
Wasp's wings are far less stunning to behold.
They lack the scales that are so bright and bold.

Wasp

Spring Peepers were singing the day
When Butterfly and Wasp flew away.
Soon Butterfly found flowers she loved best,
While Wasp began building her gray paper nest.

Wasp chews bark and wood to a pulpy paste
And then molds it into a nest to suit her taste.
Her paper nest has bands of different colors and hues
That tell which woods and barks she chose to use.

*Side view
of Butterfly*

The strange jaws of butterflies act like a straw.
From flowers sweet nectar they gently withdraw.
The jaws unfurl to drink the nectar of a flower,
Whose sugars provide them with energy and power.

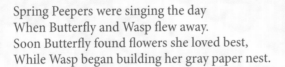
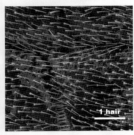

1 hair

1 hair

The overlapping scales
on Butterfly's wing

The corkscrew hairs
on Wasp's wing

1 nickel

Wasp paper

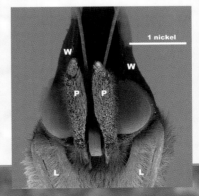

1 nickel

W

W

P P

L L

In this view of
Butterfly's face, her
jaws form a coiled
tongue (colored red)
that is surrounded
by her fuzzy eyes,
scaly palps (P),
antennae (colored
yellow), legs (L), and
raised wings (W).

As a new year unfolds, each creature sets off for new adventures along the familiar paths of…

MOUSE'S BACKYARD.

Mouse's backyard is a land of many surprises,
Where creatures come in all shapes and sizes.

Go forth, explore, and behold
How the new year will unfold.

Along familiar trails many new adventures lie
For those who venture forth to ask how and why.

To find new things, take the path you took yesterday.
–John Burroughs